COURT REPORT

Volume I

COURT REPORT

Volume I

Fran Diana Mason

IGUANA

Published by Iguana Books
720 Bathurst Street, Suite 303
Toronto, Ontario, Canada
M5V 2R4

Publisher: Greg Ioannou
Front cover image and design: Jane Awde Goodwin
Book layout design: Meghan Behse

Library and Archives Canada Cataloguing in Publication

Mason, Fran Diana, 1986-, author
        Court report : volume I / Fran Diana Mason.

Poems.
Issued in print and electronic formats.
ISBN 978-1-77180-139-3 (paperback). ISBN 978-1-77180-140-9 (epub). ISBN 978-1-77180-141-6 (kindle)

        I. Title.

PS8626.A79863C68 2015   C811'.6   C2015-906267-5
                                                 C2015-906268-3

This is an original print edition of *Court Report: Volume I.*

For D & P & K & D

Real people. Real cases.
This is *Court Report* with Fran Diana Mason.

■■

Officer, about a fight

When your partner is on the ground after having
been pushed
on his knees with his hands down
facing towards the ground
know that he was
defenceless

strikes to the head
aren't sufficient
to disengage him

drew my taser
conducted energy weapon
male continued
assaultive
crowd started to gather
in front of the entrance
exiting from the club

escalating risk increased with
the number of people
not knowing
don't know what to expect
passive
friendly
hostile
never know what you're going to get
from a crowd

opinion
that the male needed to be brought under control
because of the other potential risks
crowd that was
gathering

once he was cleared
transported
no further contact
learned his name
what he was arrested for
didn't observe
what led up
while he was struggling with the officers.

■■■

Mother, about her son at his bail hearing I

No
don't come to our house
anti-social
prison
stays home
homebody
know he's involved in music
did when he was younger
not anymore
responsibilities with 83- and 84-year-old parents
good daughter
good mother
trying to do everything
D. put heads together
intervention style
smarten up
time to

he was
he was doing it again
can't tell you what dates
worst person
taking a course for home inspections

I agree
this day in age juggle schedules
many people

fact that I live with my elderly parents
they need quiet
mini stroke.

■■

Crown, about Mr. S. the pimp

Project underway
friends were wiretapped
took texts and voice recordings
conversations
and from whoever was speaking
other person's number was checked out
during the course of the wiretaps

formed the view that there was prostitution ongoing
because of the age of the girl
arrested Mr. S.
and he went for a bail hearing
here in this court
granted bail

Mr. S. is a recognized musician
appearing with other people on Saturday

■■■

Officer, during a drunk driving trial

Traffic
light
weather
clear

6:50 a.m. stepped out of
private booth

PTA
90-days driving suspension
impound notice
copy of breath results

tell me what
where does it say

read Rights to Counsel
understood
nothing
of importance

6:27 arrived at detachment
short walk from our garage.

■■

Wife, about difficulties of attending bail hearings

Position to drop and bring
youngest
baby in the courtroom

the issue's child care
the oldest one
Xmas pageant
I took day off.

■ ■

Crown, about what police found in a bedroom

Police enter
drawer with lock
key under desk
drawer
meth
cocaine
GBH
marijuana

packaged in Ziploc
eyeglass case

desktop box
$1707, $16 in American
12g meth
11g cocaine
15g marijuana.

■ ■

Surety, being honest

Yes
job's as a maid
maid service
record check comes back

does get in the way
why I want to get pardoned.

∎∎

Crown, about a mistake

Look at the offence
robbery
serious
not belittling
shoplifting gone bad
chase after him
imitation firearm
turns out to be a lighter.

∎∎

Crown, about sentencing

Something ought to be incorporated
meaningful sentence imposed
paramount principles
protection of the public
acknowledge limited tools at your disposal.

∎∎

Judge, letting a mother speak

Judge: willing to go there
don't know what to say
- I see the mother is signalling, she wishes to
  say something:

Mother: witnessed him on this journey
respect all the information
this week he said something
good ideas
can't force him
what he said was
don't want to do drugs
makes me paranoid
crazy things.

■■

Judge, thinking out loud

Drug addiction says
not going to live to an advanced age
that's what the doctor says
without intervention
change of the lifestyle
doomed
bleak life
shorter life.

■■

Justice of the Peace, working the docket

Have to find your paperwork
save you for last
sounds good
meantime
time to organize
try again at 10:15 a.m.

■■

Crown, about a guy who now wishes he hadn't turned right

December 2
in the morning
intersection marked with 2 prohibited right-
  turn signs
sign that says you can't turn right
officer stopped the car
asked to see the driver's valid licence
vehicle proof of insurance
unable to produce DL photo card
DL has been suspended since January 7 2009
during the vehicle stop
investigation continued
disclosed to officers
possession of cocaine
weigh scale
placed under arrest and cautioned
for the possession of drugs
bundle of cash
front left pocket
white powder
2 cellphones
box of 70 plastic baggies
6.55g of cocaine.

■■

Disagreement I

Crown: record
unbroken
goes on for pages
agree with me

he didn't listen to you
words of advice
Surety: like yes and no everybody has their own
figure of speech whatever they
want to do
sometimes got to leave them to do what
they got to do
not saying it didn't work out
wife living with me too
understand what I'm saying
Crown: it's combustible
Surety: not anymore
she's gone
Crown: violence can unexpectedly spark.

■■■

**Justice of the Peace, just before the Accused
collapsed and the courtroom was cleared**

Detention ordered.

■■■

Disagreement II

Crown: any weapons in your home?
Witness: now, can I ask you a question? Why
  did you ask me that?
Crown: that's not how it works.

■■■

Officer, on Mr. B. and his home

Yellow shirt
bracelets
no one to you
initially

Tim Horton's bag with rock heroin
some quantity of heroin on his person
keys were retrieved from him
remainder of my team
used the keys to enter
Apt. 711
Mr. B.'s mother and sister
2 parties found in the living room area
small kitchen
off to the right side
hallway
2 bedrooms
end of the hallway
bathroom
right side of the hallway
Mr. B.'s bedroom was second bedroom on the left
upon entering the residence.

■■■

Defence Counsel, an apology I

Only say that I understand
frustration
made repeated efforts
explanation
that's the reason
apologize

not going to jeopardize the date of his trial
OIC
felt badly
didn't understand
he had to follow up on certain
things
apologize to Mr. C.
to the court
to Mr. P.

■■

Defence Counsel, an apology II

Expected Mr. S. to attend with me
called me to say he's a little bit ill
request a 2-week adjournment
follow-up discussion
set this down for trial come back on Thursday
January 22 please
- I apologize for my pants it was laundry day.

■■

Judge, closing remarks

32 years of age now
seems to me to be
in terms of his appearance
demeanour
closely follow what's going on in this courtroom
clear from your record that when you do get busted
end up doing your time
before you get to trial
get arrested

charged again
looking at mandatory sentences
must be a better way
to spend your life
hope you learn.

∎∎

Judge and Crown, ganging up on Mr. P.

Crown: Need some time to deal with the slightly
  changed landscape
Mr. P.'s contouring
put it that way
and given your indication
prepared to proceed

Judge: looked at the materials
Mr. P.
really out of time
terms of your service
rule requires 15 days at minimum
served in the Christmas week

Mr. P.: short fall

Judge: don't think you're addressing the issue that
  I raised
to say
why is it so late

Mr. P.: lots of trials going on
plus I had the flu
not an ideal explanation
not to make a habit of doing this sort of thing

Judge: very late filing your application
Crown hasn't had notice
or that it was even coming until literally
 days before
the application's to be heard
Crown is opposing any adjournment
application ought not to proceed
no compliance with the rule in that regard

Mr. P.: standard argument.

■■

Defence Counsel, off the record

I wanted to tell Your Honour that the
Christmas parties have never
been the same

she seems a little chunky now, you know
this is off the record
burn that Madame Reporter
burn all that.

■■

**Background on Accused, who is wearing Blue Jays
jersey**

Crown: 22 years old
was working for about 2 years
electrical apprentice
father's an electrician
5-year apprenticeship program
2 years was laid off

floating
social assistance
lived with his father
found his way into some trouble
drug-related activity
Judge: At least he likes the Blue Jays.

■■

Crown, facts of the Honey Bun Thief

Mac's convenience
Honey Buns
$1.45 each
no attempt to pay
store clerk
sidewalk
forgotten to pay
had to pay
Accused got angry
yelled
fuck off
both hands
shoved victim hard
stolen items
fell on the sidewalk.

■■

Crown, frustrated

Forces of the universe
pushing someone to do something
not actually a defence
should he go to trial

forces of the universe
not a successful defence.

■■

Judge, on the Victim Fine Surcharge

$1
no one could ever pay it.

■■

Confusion in Set Date Court

- further disclosure
- confirm receipt
- wrong brief altogether
- don't appear to have brief
- discussion with the crown
- didn't have discussion

■■

Crown, reading a charge

Theft not exceeding $5000
relates to a piece of cheese.

■■

Crown, allegations of Pita Land fight

North-east parking lot
Jane and Finch

victim walking north-east approached from behind
stated you remember me
short conversation
fuck you up
reached forward
grabbed gold chain
pulled firearm
later found to be a pellet gun
few steps back
ran in south-east direction
Pita Land Restaurant
fight ensued
Special Constable entered
detained all
not a pellet gun
Smith and Wesson model M&P .177 firearm
called his boys and stabbed and shot
difficulties in the household
father
new baby
parents under a lot of stress.

■■

Off the record

Defence Counsel: we want you to come to
    Scarborough
Justice of the Peace: my father-in-law lives in
    Scarborough, sorry I'm not coming.

■■

Crown, on the Slow Medallion Wielder

Some expenses related to the dental work
that the alleged victim reported
- I apologize Your Honour, apparently I'm stuck
  in my chair -
large medallion
swung in the air
attempt to intimidate the larger group of
people
threatening to do bodily harm
strike windshield with the medallion
further
group
during the confrontation
used his cellphone
pretended it was a firearm

in many respects private individual
forced to acknowledge his thought
process slower than many individual's
doesn't want to see himself as someone
who is incapable.

■■■

Accused, frustrated in Plea Court

Mental institution for 35 months
nothing wrong with me
I can keep going beyond the 18th
if they can't make up their mind
things get punted
I have concerns
civil wording

intent to cause
mental distress
something wrong with me
there's nothing wrong with me
Section 7
life liberty and safety
this is weighing on me like a ton of bricks
let me free of this incubus.

■■

Crown, on the Suicidal Coffee Attacker

Victim called 911 Accused returned to the
  Coffee Time
purchased a coffee exited
advanced toward the victim
removing the coffee lid threw the coffee
  victim's face

transported to 11 Division
cell number 7
chest pains needed methadone
increasingly agitated
police were concerned
attempting to hang himself with the sleeves of
his sweater.

■■

Crown, on the Suicidal Drunk Driver

One of the first hot days
of the season busy day
on the patio

brushed a vehicle
the impact though
light
drive alongside pull
over struck his vehicle
providing her driving documents
complied
observed her eyes
bloodshot
odour of alcohol
pungent
stench
evidence
her steadying herself
formed a belief
ability to operate
was impaired

place a call to DC
attempts to call Mr. P.
unsuccessful
11:50 p.m.
spoke with DC
11:56
suitable sample obtained
second sample
due course
upon her arrival at traffic
services
black jumpsuit to orange

suicidal tendencies
long black laces which police thought
might use to harm herself
date that she had last seen
her mother

died three years previous
grandfather had died in her arms
a number of years previous
on the same date
suicidal tendencies
returning from work
so upset pulled into a laneway
and sobbed because of memories attached.

■■■

Drug Treatment Court, clapping

Any use?
- no use (clapping)
Any use?
- just marijuana
Any use?
- Tylenol 3 and Suboxone and Saturday and
Sunday alcohol marijuana cocaine on Friday
and alcohol on Friday
Any use?
- Friday marijuana and cocaine
Any use?
- Crystal meth and heroin all week
Any use?
- Monday was marijuana every day glass of
wine Thursday crack and marijuana shot of
sambuca marijuana daily glass of wine
yesterday
Any use?
- Tylenol 1s and 3 a day and 2 Tylenol this morning
Any use?
- Marijuana Saturday and Sunday
Any use?

- Thursday Friday Saturday cocaine and alcohol
Any use?
- No use (clapping)
Any use?
- Friday and Saturday crack and weed
Any use?
- No use since I reported marijuana a week ago
(clapping)
Any use?
- Yesterday marijuana
Any use?
- No use (clapping)
Any use?
- Marijuana daily and Tylenol 1 for my tooth and
Friday and Saturday unprescribed sleeping pills
Any use?
- Yesterday marijuana and cocaine
Any use?
- Friday was heroin and OxyContin
Any use?
- Saturday was cocaine and Clonazepan marijuana
yesterday and alcohol
Any use?
- Cocaine and alcohol last night and this morning
Any use?
- Sunday marijuana and cocaine

■■■

Crown, being nice

Screened for some hours of community service
hip surgery resulted in an infection
not in a position to do any community service
original allegations involves a theft of a cane

amount involved was small
content the charge be withdrawn.

■■

Crown, blabbing in Set Date Court

Reminder slip says 9
says 9 today
happens
don't have his brief
shouldn't be work full-time go to school at night
come back on Wednesday morning
need three weeks
810 before the court
810 before the court
like an opportunity to explain

don't have that information
no message
have it on scope for 102 court
call 102 to confirm
proper in 102
on an error.

■■

Zanta and Justice of the Peace, on Zanta's Santa hat

Zanta: only keeping my Santa hat on
in respect took my red hat off
so I wouldn't
shine in your eyes
winter hat
insecure about my head

Justice of the Peace: that's fine he can keep
  his hat on
Zanta: everyone here
google ZANTA
daughter Amy made me famous.

■■

Defence Counsel, being sassy

Judge: which gentleman do you have on file today?
Defence Counsel: he's not a gentleman but
  it's Mr. M.

■■

Accused, being creepy

See you this weekend.

■■

Accused, from lockdown

Yeah
and tell my lawyer I
can't call her
lockdown everyday.

■■

Defence Counsel, on his client

Hero
really been trying to
better himself
what else to say
he's trying.

■■■

Mother, about her son at his bail hearing II

Could give him 24
hour supervision
always home
do random checks
wherever
the room
his clothing
pockets
I could do that.
He's not going to go back to drugs
be more participating
family
community
church
more good things.

■■■

Defence Counsel, earning his money

See that he appears to be emotional
tears coming from this man's eyes
that is remorse

where he may go
give the court some confidence
can and will obey the court's orders
that will keep him on the straight and narrow.

■■

Just before Accused has a seizure

Accused: Been in custody for 2 months
epilepsy have not had any medication in 2 months
jail has been refusing to give me any of my
  medication
can't handle all of this
stress of not having
Justice of the Peace: Hang on a second give
  me a moment spoken with your lawyer take a
  deep breath can write on your order of
  remand getting your information can
  understand upset suggest take a minute to
  call might need medical attention
(Accused having seizure)
Justice of the Peace: call for medical
  attention now.

■■

Crown, allegations of sex assault in car repair shop

Complainant brought her car
transmission repair
spoke with Accused works there
advise require 4 hours to complete repairs
asked financial quote said pay for it with kiss

Complainant believed joking
Accused provided estimate
left
come back to pick up vehicle
observed Accused front asked if ready
advised it was
escorted inside locked
main glass entry doors
escorted private office locked behind
seeing he had locked doors
Complainant ask vehicle repairs
Accused said I told you pay me kiss
grabbed upper arm pulled her body closer
attempting to kiss her
recoiled
asked again what he was doing
told you pay me with kiss
told Accused never agreed
approached and grabbed face
pushed body against
tried to kiss her on the mouth
picked up cellphone pretended to receive call
  from father
saw police
flagged them down gave statement
no injuries sustained.

■■■

Disagreement III

- new charge
- don't have no charge no cop came up and charged me
- incident relates coffee being thrown
- bring me here spilled some coffee on somebody

■■■

Disagreement IV

Defence Counsel: understand what's going on say
  don't understand
Accused: yep yep.

■■

Crown, facts on the Casino Boxer

OLG slots notified surveillance team
slot machine G3907 was broken
reviewed investigation 2 hours prior
10:15 that night male person, Accused, punched
the main screen
right fist
exited gaming floor
tests conducted on the machine confirmed
  monitor
cracked needed to be replaced
monitor taped
slot machine taken out of service
total repair cost $1203.45.

■■

Court Clerk, a correction

Spelled 'Dronald'
actually 'Ronald.'

■■

Crown, on Mr. Divine

Have disclosure for Mr. Divine
Mr. Divine a starting point
sort that out Mr. Divine
myself and Mr. Divine increases time
make sure Mr. Divine
seen those videos
Mr. Divine receiving same
never had a Crown Pretrial
with Mr. Divine
asked
said yes I did.

■■■

Defence Counsel, grateful

On that footing
crown prepared
internal
interpretation of time served
sign it
say something
show it to the crown
go outside for a moment
need some time
God bless you.

■■■

Crown, on a double death

No fixed address
why he might be residing in a storage locker

when he died
he died.

■■■

**Accused, on where he was living before his
arrest**

I think in October he died
he told me before I went to jail
when I went to jail got out of jail
that's when the super told me
person who used to live there died

can't sleep too much on that bed
the smell of paint
I can smell all the paint

I would sleep in the pantry room
I would sleep on the sofa in the party room
couldn't sleep with the paint

that guy
person who worked there died
probably because he was sleeping there
really can't take the smell

slept in the workshop
sleep there not spend overnight there
don't want to sleep there because somebody
  died there
have slept there
yes I have slept there
but smell of the paint can't take the smell of
  the paint

that's why
don't want to stay there all the time
all smells of paint.

■■■

**Defence Counsel, on the background of their
client I**

No fixed address since 15 years of age
mother in nursing home since 15 years old
worked odd jobs
hasn't had any permanent kind of employment
ODSP since 25
does suffer schizophrenia
diagnosed at 25
related offences on there
more of a record
of someone who has been living on the
  streets
does suffer from PTSD from witnessing a murder
at 24 years of age.

■■■

Crown, withdrawing a charge

Accused deceased
charge withdrawn.

■■■

**Defence Counsel, on the background of their
client II**

32 from the area reservation
Native has 5 brothers
4 actually and 1 sister
tragic
the father was an alcoholic
violent
father went looking
for the mother with a shotgun
believed mother in the outhouse
blew away the outhouse
trying to kill the mother
father was murdered
mother died
drowned
investigation
foul play

PSR prepared
all the children adopted by a non-native family
  quite a handsome government stipend for each
$2900/month for having these children
own children got good clothes fed well
adopted children used clothes not very good food
left age 16.

■■

Disagreement V

Judge: strike the plea
Accused: want it done today
pled guilty said I went into the store

don't understand
Judge: said a variety of things
not accepting your guilty plea
Accused: want to plead guilty
in the store under my will
went into the store
told the police officer said yes sir
took me in plead guilty in the store
went in the store
shouldn't have gone in the store
in the store
pleading wasn't asking anyone for change was in
  the store
don't understand pleading guilty
camera there pleading guilty to being in the store
was in the store
Judge: remand to February 4
Accused: let it be done today got up 3 mornings
  in a row to come here
Judge: February 4.

■■

**Accused, on screen in court from the Video
Remand Room at jail**

Legal Aid case #236
victim police corruption
5th lawyer
victim white collar crime
contact Prime Minister of this country
captain of this jail is a psychopath
all of my lawyers victims of police corruption
white collar crime
first lawyer suspended

second lawyer suspended
four previous lawyers all fired
middle of an appeal process
Legal Aid 2380129 contacted Prime Minister
of this country
have his address contacting Ontario Premier
called the RCMP approximately 500 times
Happy Valentine's.

■■■

Defence Counsel, on the background of their client III

57 Canadian 1 wife deceased
5 sisters
2 brothers
born in Toronto
unemployed 20 plus years
severe alcohol
depression issues
wife deceased
murdered
1985
since then hard on him spiralled out of control.

■■■

Crown, on an alleged attack by Accused in a shelter

Ended up face to face
staff member
so close he caused the staff member's
glasses to fog up.

■■

Disagreement VI

Judge: assaulted V.?
Accused: ran up behind me
didn't hurt anybody
came up behind me turned around
dropped my bottle ran, sir
didn't assault anybody no.
Crown: if Accused not willing to agree assault
  with a weapon
Judge: can't take your plea on that
Accused: large cheque at stake waiting don't have time
take anything plead guilty to 4 months
Judge: number of years ago appointed judge of
  the court
swore to be a judge
legally
and morally can't say "look, Smith says he
  didn't do it"
innocent man to plead guilty pretend to be guilty
can't do it
Accused: what is going on
have a large cheque waiting for me at home
don't understand
ready to get out of here
Judge: don't take pleas from innocent people and
  sentence them.

■■

Accused, standing alone in Plea Court

Change my life conclusion
do shit on my own
trying to do it on my own
need some help
at this time in my life
fear is one of them
young son
love to be his father
recently
haven't seen much
get into program
once I get in
won't see much of him again.

∎∎∎

Accused, sitting in his wheelchair alone in Plea Court

Yes so happy whatever you say waiting for
  your decision and God that is all no family
  here only the Law and God.

∎∎∎

The Esso Gas Station Stalker

Accused: bow to Your Honour
Duty Counsel: don't have any concerns about
  fitness today.

∎∎∎

The woman who wanted to kill her boyfriend

Crown: distraught
cheating on her
Accused noticed couple men smoking
inquired
arranged boyfriend physically assaulted
price $3500
Defence Counsel: Ask for some kind of term
  allowing her to attend gym rather than staying
  entirely in her apartment.

■■

Crown, on Mr. W's garage

Left the scene of the assault
drove home stopping
convenience
continued went home
left the phone outside
got something to eat
last part of that not true
when he does go home
goes into the garage
takes recycling out

testified
bought the coke from Frankie
took drugs back to girlfriend's house
did tests
return it because it was bad didn't want to leave it
took it over to dad's house
sister answered
went to the garage

put the bag with the drugs under hood of the
  Honda

red shirt coming back
look at the garage door
go inside
final video
where R.W. comes to the door
rings the bell
waits on the steps
leaves lights to the car
flash

Mr. W. comes out of the garage
male early teens
holding a flashlight
moves Honda
driveway to the street
followed by the van
both go back into the garage

Mr. W. pulls out lawnmower
of the garage side of property
back to the garage
backs out dark coloured car

that dark car
both friend and I agree BMW
pulls out of the garage
parks road
Mr. W. parks the van
partway in the driveway
puts the lawnmower
back into the garage
backs partway
into garage

6:30 in the morning
exits the front door
coffee mug
driver's side Honda
dark car BMW
no longer parked out front that morning

at 7:03 a.m. Honda pulls back
goes in front carrying paper
and a bag
comes back out empty handed
passenger side van front of the Honda
backs out of the driveway again

at 10:19 a.m. Honda pulls back
into the driveway
Mr. W. gets out plastic bag
front of the van front door
exits the front door
gets back into the driver's seat
Honda

that night
little girl comes up the stairs
followed by Mr. W.
parked in driveway
go inside the house

11:43 a.m. Honda pulls into garage
Mr. W. walks down the driveway
goes into garage

11:57 a.m. the van backs into the driveway
Mr. W. exits the van
opens the tailgate
loads various items
garage to trunk of van.

■■

Disagreement VII

Crown: breach probation charge
placed probation
one of the terms
not to possess any weapons
Accused: I never carry any weapons
Crown: walking cane converted used as a weapon.

■■

Fight with Roommate Guy, grateful he's not being sent to jail

Judge: effusive with the court
meaning
he has said on many occasions
things like thank you my Lord
elevated this court way beyond
where it should be
Accused: I wish this kind of justice would
 have existed in my home country I would have
 never left really appreciate the fairness
 justice I'm receiving
Judge: no one is asking for thanks
part of the job of doing justice
Accused: try to imagine how I feel someone
 like you ask me how am I doing have nobody
 to check for me that means a lot.

■■

Crown, on Accused who broke the conditions of his probation

Seated at the bar
drinking brandy
challenge officers
for entering
showing signs intoxication
blatant breach
sitting in a bar
intoxicated.

■■

Crown, on the trickster Mr. B.

Fail to Appear Fail To Comply again and
  again
cannot have confidence
plan proposed hoping
based on hope
B. Senior hoping son change
everybody hopes
have to go on more than hope
surveillance for those offences
fake fire alarm extinguisher inspector
looks remarkably like Mr. B.

■■

Accused, at his bail hearing

Only surety here my brother and he's dying
  of cancer.

■■

Disagreement VIII

Duty Counsel: ask warrant be marked for
  medical attention
dehydration
Justice of the Peace: question of hydration
  give him some water hydration issue needs
  some water.

■■

Disagreement IX

Accused: what are the charges read the charges
Crown: (reads charges)
Accused: fucking bullshit
when I was at the station
it was fucking theft under and resist arrest
that's all it was
you guys got your paperwork messed up
ok?

■■

**Crown, allegations against the man who
threatened to harm his own dog**

She's with him at home address
parents Chinese New Year that evening
began arguing
he grabbed her arm
dragged her
trying to bring her upstairs
crying
then on Wednesday at the mall

Eaton Centre
conversation outside Apple store
became upset
grabbed her neck
pushed her head down
ground
dragged her
no injuries
relationship over
continued to text
phone asking her to reconcile
indicated wreak havoc
unregister her from online classes
threatened to harm his own dog
if she didn't respond
text: you better call me
don't let me find you
find you
wait to die.

■■

Mother, about her son at his bail hearing III

In addition to conditions proposed
ask court to add condition
arrive home early
spend more time family.

■■

Justice of the Peace, about jail and the courts

Host,
Majesty the Queen,
not the best.

■■

Accused, on why he can't do his bail hearing today

Jail on my birthday came here change my life
- where fiancee
staying shelter no way getting a hold of her
  dialysis for her kidneys.

■■

The Uncertain Hooch Thief

Court Clerk: how do you plead guilty or not guilty?
Accused: guilty...except
Defence Counsel: indulgence
ensure client pleading properly
may have to hold down
you don't want to plea
we'll have a trial
Accused: I'm guilty, I guess
Defence Counsel: there's no I guess, Your
  Honour I think we may have to hold it down
prepared rely facts as disclosed
Crown: (reads fact)
Defence Counsel: is that correct Mr. L.?
tried to steal the booze? what he just read
about the Crown Royal?
Accused: suppose it's correct
Judge: drinking that day?
Accused: probably
Defence Counsel: subject to Your Honour
Defence Counsel: Sammy, did you steal the alcohol?

Accused: well, I must of
Defence Counsel: subject to Your Honour
Crown: games he's playing
Defence Counsel: he's not playing games
many medical issues
constellation of health issues
memory fractured.

∎∎∎

The Healthy Witness

Crown: know anything about drugs?
Witness: professional sports my country
  Paris, France
can't smoke cigarettes, never smoke
Crown: know what drugs look like? cutting agent?
Witness: drink milk everyday 35 years strong man.

∎∎∎

Pre-Enquete Prattle by the Informant

Mr. T. trusted as a friend
fallen out
the war on Bloor Street
day that Whitney Houston passed away
became friends again
able to sit down
4 broken bones
right foot
habit of falling
equilibrium issue
bad luck

that morning
drinking all night
going on about Cartier watch
father's ring
knows I'm a bloodhound
spent the morning looking for her watch
meeting
the rich lesbian couple
vodka shooters
said have one
teeny-wee sip
celebrate when I get home
dining room table
you can have it
give you half proceeds
Cartier
when I pawn it

sexually and criminally harassed
do things
not appropriate
put it that way
discrimination coming out the yin yang

own 3 original Picassos
Renoirs
store somewhere very safe
used to be very well off
assets
can't sell
take to New York
Christie's to do it

pieces
mother
grandmother
mother's house

helped me clean it out
promised hold onto my jewellery for me
huge collection
antique dishes from 1700
few pieces I've travelled internationally
confirmed by a number of individuals
who work for the UN
who've been to my various homes
ex-judges know me personally

can't see my daughter
get some of my funds back
up for some great jobs right now
data systems
PhD computer engineering Stanford
KPNG Offshore
used to be in offshore banking
TD Canada Trust
created my own company.

■■■

Q & A, money and two pairs of pants

Crown: what did you do?
Witness: secured other hand searched locate
  other property
Crown: describe search
Witness: two pairs of pants inner pair located
2 five dollar bills
condoms
cigars
set of keys
piece of paper
quantity cash folded over not in sequence

also located cellphone
Crown: what did you do with that money?
Witness: evidence money
count it complete proper paperwork count it
6 twenties 2 fifties 8 more twenties 1 fifty
  1 of the twenties older twenty not circulation
  2 five dollar bills
$440 Canadian
photocopied it forms photographed sealed
  submitted property evidence locker 33
Defence Counsel: oet's talk about the outer
  pair of pants
Witness: jeans
Defence Counsel: belt on?
Witness: don't recall
Defence Counsel: baggy or tighter?
Witness: baggy
Defence Counsel: inner pair pants how would you
  describe?
Witness: track pants
Defence Counsel: colour?
Witness: dark blue didn't make notes
Defence Counsel: tight? loose fitting?
Witness: wasn't focused type of pants was
  what was inside the pants
Defence Counsel: how many pockets?

■ ■

Sadism Likely

Crown: hospital records
concern expressed
serious violence
pleasure ripping open animals while they were alive

fantasizes doing this to people
paranoid antisocial.

■■

Reasons given for missing court

single mother
money problems
2 kids
incarcerated
identity theft
illness
student
lawyer didn't write down right date
tragic circumstances
sick
out of the country
73 years old not aware of the process
family emergency
forgot the date
hospital extended period of time
house arrest for 5 years
brother went to wrong courtroom
newborn stress
fatality on 401
out of country in Pakistan right now
daughter sick
colon and pancreas problems
hospitalized
got a call from a specialist and had to take the
  appointment
taking mother for hip replacement.

■■

Witness, on the contents of her patient's medicine cabinet

Gabapentin 200mg twice a day for neck pain
Mirtazapine for depression and anxiety
Venlafaxine 75mg daily for depression
Bupropion antidepressant
Vyvanse 40mg for ADHD
Nortriptyline 4 capsules at bedtime
Olanzapine 15mg 2 tablets an antipsychotic mood
  stabilizer
Clonidine to help lower blood pressure.

www.ingramcontent.com/pod-product-compliance
Lightning Source LLC
Chambersburg PA
CBHW032131050726
47590CB00008B/3036